ALFRED's
CRED PERFORMER
OLLECTIONS

Sunday Morning *Holiday* Companion

33 Timeless Selections for Worship Throughout the Year

Arranged by Victor Labenske

Sunday Morning Holiday Companion provides 33 accessible arrangements that are appropriate for the holiday seasons throughout the year. Included are selections for Lent, Holy Week, Easter, Pentecost, Reformation Sunday, Thanksgiving, and Christmas. Several patriotic titles are included as well. The arrangements require minimal preparation time for the busy church pianist. To assist in planning, approximate performance times are included for each piece. My goal in writing this collection was to create interesting arrangements that explore a variety of traditional and contemporary styles, while providing music that is both worshipful and appropriate for church use.

D1710682

Alfred

Alphabetical Contents

(Approx. Performance Time – 1:45)

HALLELUJAH! WHAT A SAVIOR!

Philip P. Bliss
Arr. Victor Labenske

(Approx. Performance Time – 3:15)

JESUS PAID IT ALL

John T. Grape
Arr. Victor Labenske

*Prelude
4-6-14*

(Approx. Performance Time – 2:30)

NEAR THE CROSS

William H. Doane
Arr. Victor Labenske

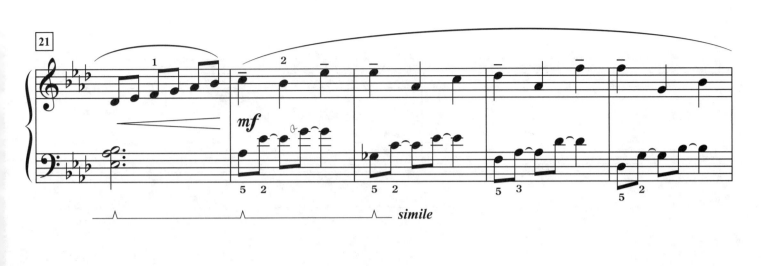

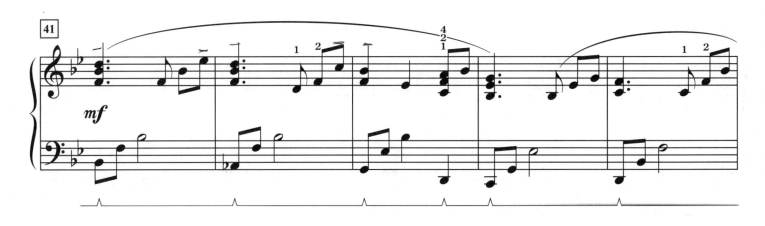

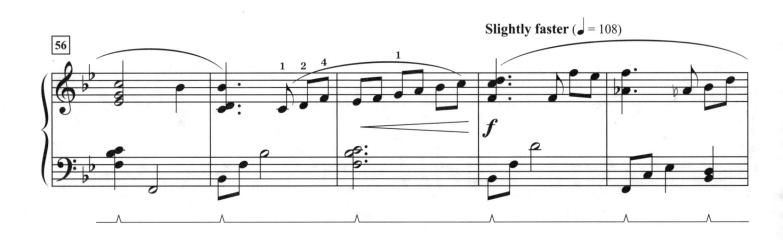

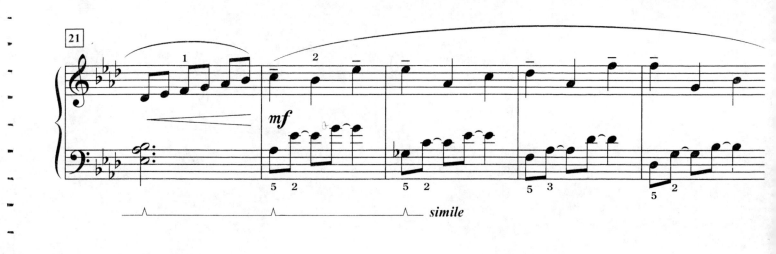

(Approx. Performance Time – 3:30)

THERE IS A FOUNTAIN

Traditional American Melody
Arr. Victor Labenske

(Approx. Performance Time – 2:15)

THE WAY OF THE CROSS LEADS HOME

Charles H. Gabriel
Arr. Victor Labenske

(Approx. Performance Time – 3:00)

AT THE CROSS

Ralph E. Hudson
Arr. Victor Labenske

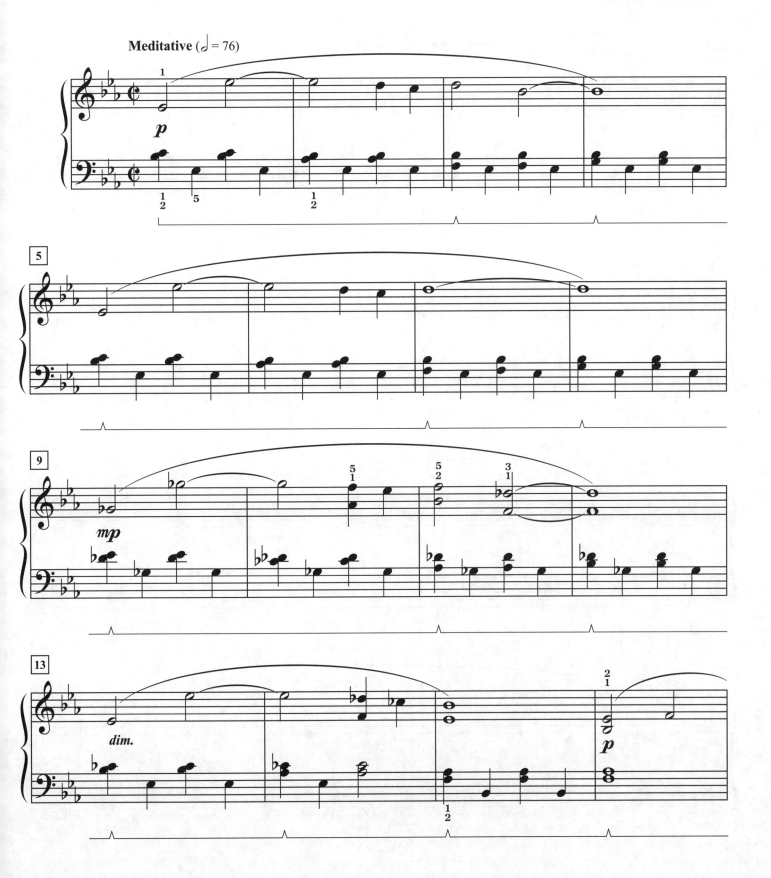

(Approx. Performance Time – 1:45)

ALL GLORY, LAUD AND HONOR

Melchior Teschner
Arr. Victor Labenske

(Approx. Performance Time – 2:30)

GO TO DARK GETHSEMANE

Richard Redhead
Arr. Victor Labenske

(Approx. Performance Time – 2:15)

LEAD ME TO CALVARY

William J. Kirkpatrick
Arr. Victor Labenske

(Approx. Performance Time – 2:15)

HOSANNA, LOUD HOSANNA

Gesängbuch der Herzogl
Arr. Victor Labenske

(Approx. Performance Time – 2:30)

WHAT WONDROUS LOVE IS THIS?

William Walker
Arr. Victor Labenske

(Approx. Performance Time – 2:30)

CHRIST AROSE

Robert Lowry
Arr. Victor Labenske

(Approx. Performance Time – 2:00)

CHRIST THE LORD IS RISEN TODAY, ALLELUIA

Traditional
Arr. Victor Labenske

With rubato (♩ = ca. 126)

mp

(Approx. Performance Time — 1:45)

Dedicated to Karlin Labenske

THE DAY OF RESURRECTION

Henry Smart
Arr. Victor Labenske

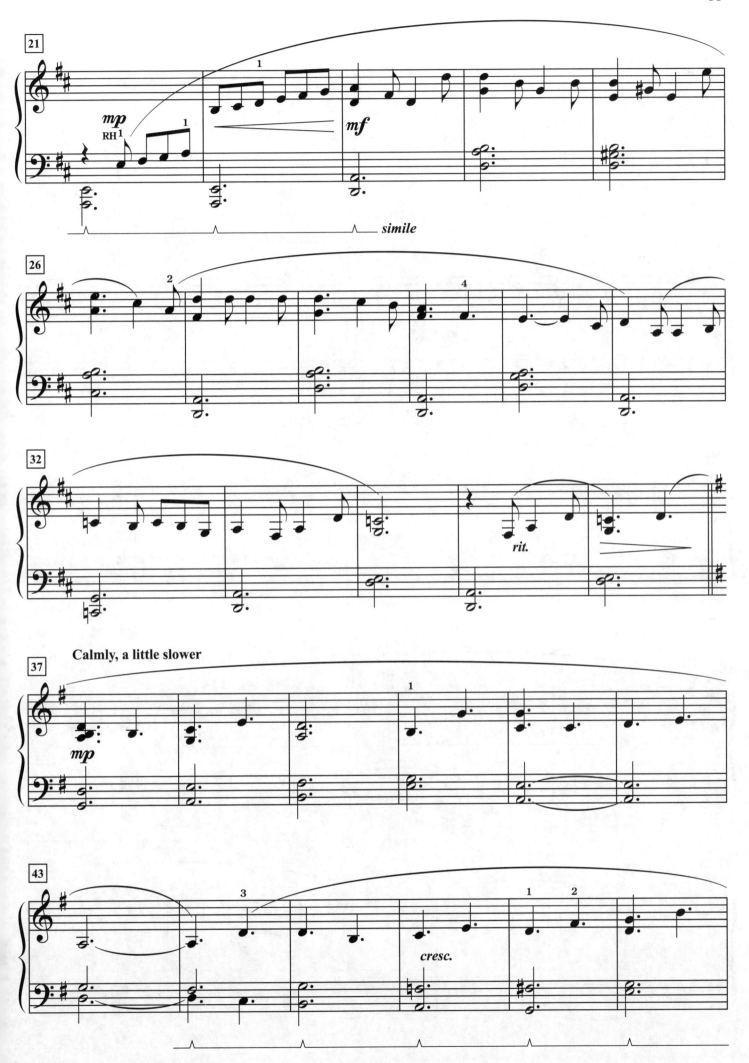

54

(Approx. Performance Time – 2:30)

CHRIST THE LORD IS RISEN TODAY

Lyra Davidica
Arr. Victor Labenske

(Approx. Performance Time – 1:45)

BREATHE ON ME, BREATH OF GOD

Robert Jackson
Arr. Victor Labenske

(Approx. Performance Time – 2:30)

THE COMFORTER HAS COME

William J. Kirkpatrick
Arr. Victor Labenske

(Approx. Performance Time – 3:00)

SPIRIT OF GOD, DESCEND UPON MY HEART

Frederick C. Atkinson
Arr. Victor Labenske

(Approx. Performance Time – 2:00)

BATTLE HYMN OF THE REPUBLIC

Traditional American Melody
Arr. Victor Labenske

(Approx. Performance Time – 2:00)

GOD OF OUR FATHERS

George W. Warren
Arr. Victor Labenske

Prelude 7-3-14

(Approx. Performance Time – 2:30)

AMERICA THE BEAUTIFUL

Samuel A. Ward
Arr. Victor Labenske

(Approx. Performance Time – 2:15)

MY COUNTRY 'TIS OF THEE

Traditional
Arr. Victor Labenske

Slightly broader (♩ = 116)

(Approx. Performance Time – 2:30)

O CANADA!

Calixa Lavallée
Arr. Victor Labenske

(Approx. Performance Time – 2:00)

THE STAR-SPANGLED BANNER

John Stafford Smith
Arr. Victor Labenske

I Love Thy Kingdom, Lord

Aaron Williams
Arr. Victor Labenske

(Approx. Performance Time – 1:45)

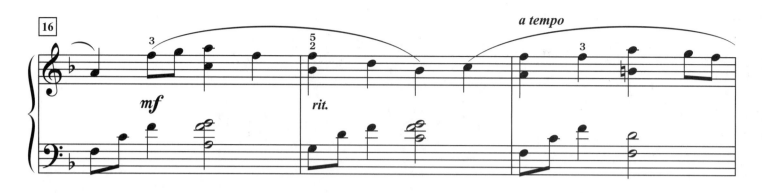

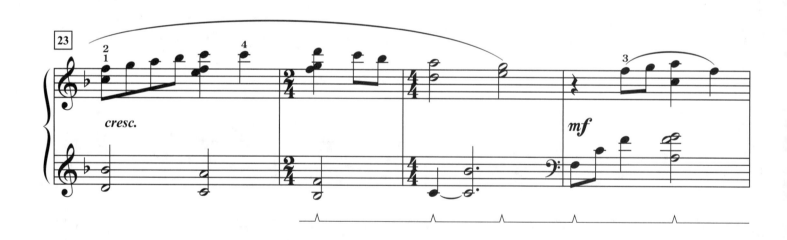

(Approx. Performance Time – 2:15)

THE CHURCH'S ONE FOUNDATION

Samuel S. Wesley
Arr. Victor Labenske

Fast and rhythmic ($\quad$ = 132)

(Approx. Performance Time – 3:00)

THE SOLID ROCK

William B. Bradbury
Arr. Victor Labenske

(Approx. Performance Time – 2:15)

COME, YE THANKFUL PEOPLE, COME

George J. Elvey
Arr. Victor Labenske

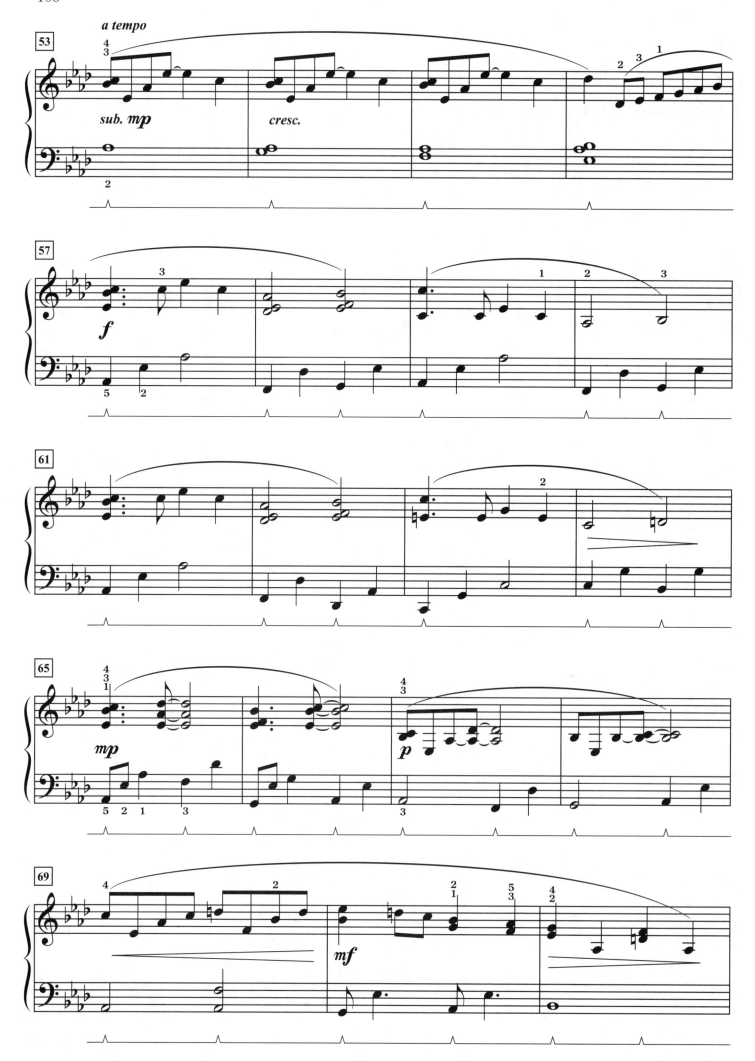

Prelude 11/3/13

(Approx. Performance Time – 2:15)

COUNT YOUR BLESSINGS

Edwin O. Excell
Arr. Victor Labenske

(Approx. Performance Time – 1:45)

LET ALL THINGS NOW LIVING

Traditional Welsh Melody
Arr. Victor Labenske

(Approx. Performance Time – 2:15)

Now Thank We All Our God

Johann Crueger
Arr. Victor Labenske

intro.

rit. e dim.

(Approx. Performance Time – 1:45)

Dedicated to Kristofer Labenske

ON CHRISTMAS NIGHT ALL CHRISTIANS SING
(SUSSEX CAROL)

Traditional English Carol
Arr. Victor Labenske

(Approx. Performance Time – 2:15)

IT CAME UPON THE MIDNIGHT CLEAR

Richard S. Willis
Arr. Victor Labenske

128